10 easy ways to earn money from facebook

Deepak Yadav

pencil

ISBN 978-93-5610-982-7
© Deepak Yadav 2022
Published in India 2022 by Pencil

A brand of

One Point Six Technologies Pvt. Ltd.
123, Building J2, Shram Seva Premises,
Wadala Truck Terminal, Wadala (E)
Mumbai 400037, Maharashtra, INDIA
E connect@thepencilapp.com
W www.thepencilapp.com

DISCLAIMER: *The opinions expressed in this book are those of the authors and do not purport to reflect the views of the Publisher.*

Author biography

I am an infopreneur and i make money online.

I have seen many ups and downs in my life.

But the year 2016 was the worst time of my life because at this time I was very much troubled by depression and anxiety.

I made every effort to get out of this mental state.

Today I am far away from depression and anxiety.

In fact my life changed after the depression.

I learned many life lessons during this time and I want to teach this lesson to you through my books.

I hope you get to learn a lot from my books which might change your career and life.

CONTENTS

Preface

Do you use internet?

If yes, then you must be aware of Facebook.

Have you ever used a like or share service on Facebook?

If yes then you would know how popular it is.

Do you know that you can also earn money using this platform?

If not, then you are not using the social media platform properly.

Facebook, which is the choice of millions of people, which is used by every person today, which is a popular social media site, it is not only a means of entertainment but also a great way of earning.

The mobile or laptop which has internet, the user of that mobile and laptop does not know Facebook, this cannot happen, but very few people know that money can also be earned from Facebook.

Many people will be surprised to hear this but it is true and in today's post we are going to tell you about the ways by which you can earn money using Facebook.

We often put our pictures or any other post on Facebook and we also enjoy a lot in this work.

Just imagine, how would it feel if you started getting money while doing this fun job?

Facebook is a platform that we use every day.

Sometimes it is a great platform for entertainment to share your own posts or to like other's posts or to watch funny videos.

Facebook has become an important part of the social network through which you can connect with your friends, relatives as well as new people online.

It is a way to connect with each other.

Facebook is a completely free platform in which we only have to create an account and after that we can use it as much as we want, so Facebook becomes a great way to earn money, under this you will get such features which if you have learned to use then understand that you took one step on the ladder of success

But one thing you should know that for every work you do not get money from Facebook, that is, if you think that you will do anything and you will get money then you are wrong.

If you are thinking that Facebook will ever give you money, then it is not so, but by using it you can earn money and today we are going to tell you about these methods, then stay connected to our blog till the end.

There are millions of people connected on Facebook whom you can easily reach.

Who needs to make money from Facebook?

This question must have come in the mind of many people that it is okay to earn from Facebook, but what things will be required for this?

So you don't need to worry you don't have to worry about using Facebook, it is absolutely free, all you need is a laptop or mobile and a good internet connection connected to it.

Apart from this, what is most important is maximum audience, because without them you cannot be successful in this field.

The more audience you have, the more you will be in profit, here you are being given a proper list, which you will need in this platform-

1. Smartphone or Laptop

2. Internet connection

3. Facebook Account

4. Facebook Groups

5. Patience

Now here comes the first thing that how do we increase the followers on our Facebook account or Facebook page means how to increase the audience because without this we cannot do our work further.

So first of all you have to add many people to your account, about 1000 to 10000 people.

For this, you will find many features on Facebook which will help you to contact people.

With their help, you can easily connect with people and increase followers on your account.

For example, there is a way – Facebook Groups.

Where the task of collecting followers becomes easy.

You can either join the group created by people first and increase your followers by posting there or you can join with many people by creating a group from Facebook account.

Another way is Facebook page.

Where the task of increasing the audience is a bit difficult, but if you increase the followers in this way, then it will be easy for you to earn money from Facebook.

The third way is buy or sell group (buy and sell group).

If even after trying a lot, you are not gathering enough followers that you can proceed with your work, then you can join with many people by opening a Facebook account and going to the Facebook Buy and Sell group, that is, buying the group and contacting people. can do.

Here you will find many groups which are available for sale, so in this way your work becomes easy, although you have to pay money for this.

Now you have got all kinds of knowledge about what you need to have and how you can get it.

So let us now tell you the 10 easiest ways to earn money from Facebook, using which you can also earn online and join digital marketing-

1. Earn money by showing ads on Facebook-

Today's era is full of advertisements whether it is television or mobile or laptop, everywhere you get to see some kind of ads.

But have you ever thought that what can be the benefit to the front by showing the ad?

If not, then you will be surprised to know that by showing these advertisements companies earn up to lakhs of rupees and this is an easy and best way to earn money.

You can also do this work through Facebook and earn a lot of money.

For this neither you need any degree nor you should have knowledge of ad and facebook to put more mind.

You can create a lot of money by using your free time.

As you know that advertising is a method of promotion of any product or service, which is used by even the smallest companies.

There are many ways to earn money through ads, in which you can earn money by placing ads, you can earn money by showing ads, even you can earn money by watching ads.

If you have a lot of traffic on your Facebook account, that means you have a large audience, then you can show ads on your account.

For this there is a famous company which is known as Google Adsense and it is a completely secure company that pays you money for showing ads.

But this does not mean that anyone can use it, for this you have to have an audience.

Let us tell you about this with an example-

Suppose your company is about to launch a new product that you want to promote or a company gives you a project to promote its new product.

So in such a situation, you will create an ad by advertising on Facebook, under which you have to decide for how many days you will run this promotion, this is called an ad campaign which is done for a limited time.

Under Facebook, you will find an Ads Manager platform within which you can create and publish ads.

First of all, you have to login to your Facebook account and go to the dropdown-menu of the account.

After going there you will get the option of Create Add or Manage Add.

By clicking on the option of create add, you will be taken to a page where you have to enter your account name and create account.

You will also get a guide as you progress.

After this, the main page of Facebook and Creation will open in front of you where you will get many options to create an ad.

You can start an ad campaign by creating your own ad.

Here different types of options will help you to do different promotion like if you want to make your product name famous then you can choose awareness and if you want traffic on your website then you can choose traffic.

You will find many such options.

To start this work, first you have to choose the marketing objective.

When you have created an account in the section containing your ad, first you have to choose the objective under it such as Awareness, Conversions or Traffic.

After this you will get the next option to set up the add in which basically you have to define things like limit and budget of the add.

After setting up the ad, you choose the audience which is according to the location and under this you have to decide under which place you want to show your ad.

Here you can set the interest that your ad will show to people who will search about it or are interested in it.

Under this, you will also know how many people your ads can reach.

After this you can set your budget how much money you want to spend on this ad campaign.

If you want, you can pay it daily or you can also set it to basic for the week.

After this, you get the option to create an ad, in which you can create an ad or can also choose a post from a Facebook page as an ad.

Keep in mind that you have to share the link of the Facebook page with every ad because Facebook will show your ad only if you have linked the Facebook page.

Then you choose the format of the ad and complete your work by uploading images and videos etc.

All this work depends on the marketing objectives because according to that the links etc.

Inside each option, you will find many options which will help you to customize.

When all your work is completed, you can submit your ad for review.

If you get approval on Facebook, then you reach people according to a schedule.

You can also easily view its result and export it.

In this way, you can promote your product by putting a small cost for the ad and the more people who buy your product through that ad, the more commission you will get.

2. Earn Money Through Facebook Affiliate Marketing-

You must have heard the name of affiliate marketing, it is the biggest form of digital marketing.

But very few people know how much you can get by doing affiliate marketing with Facebook.

In Affiliate Marketing, you can sell any product through Facebook.

By selling more and more products, you get more commission and higher will be your income.

It is very easy to do it just you need some patience for this because no work can be done overnight.

If you are engaged on Facebook all day long then you have a good chance to earn money through Affiliate Marketing.

In today's time Facebook has become the number one social networking site in the world.

Therefore, affiliate marketing through Facebook becomes a powerful tool from which you can earn a lot of money sitting at home.

In Affiliate Marketing, you have to sell any of your products.

If you are looking to start your new business and want to do affiliate marketing through Facebook, then choose a product that will increase your sales.

For this, you will find many groups easily available on Facebook, through which you can be a part of affiliate marketing, such as - Amazon and Flipkart.

To earn money from affiliate marketing, first you have to create an account on the affiliate network, under which you get the option of Amazon Affiliate Account and Flipkart Affiliate Account.

From here you can get the affiliate link of any product you want and copy the URL address of that product to open your account.

After this, paste the URL of the product by clicking on the option of affiliate link generator and click on OK to generate this link.

After doing this you can share this link on Facebook

With this you can promote Affiliate Marketing on Facebook, for which the gender of Affiliate Marketing has to be promoted.

Because on social media you will find many affiliate programs that give you commission for doing so.

For this, you have to join the affiliate program and it is not necessary that you join only one program, if you want, you can join many programs simultaneously.

After joining a program, you get a link to the affiliate program, which can have many types of services.

It can contain any service related to the product or business and if you share it from your account or share it on your page

So all the people who click on this link and buy the product, you will get their commission and as the sales increase, so will your income.

There is no limit to earn commission in affiliate marketing.

This is a work that depends on the sale of the product you send and the best part is that you do not have to buy any product for this, you only promote the service of the people.

For this, you have to take care of some things like first of all you have to choose a better affiliate program as well as a product that can fetch you high commission.

From time to time, you can also share many offers on your Facebook account with the link.

This is a great tool for your Facebook affiliate marketing.

Now let us tell you what can be the best affiliate marketing option on Facebook?

That is a blog or a website.

Many bloggers earn money by doing affiliate marketing like this, so if you join them and promote their blog or website on your Facebook account, then you can benefit more from it.

If you want, you can also promote your own block by joining the affiliate program.

Keep in mind that you write a review of every product or service well so that more and more people are attracted to you.

3. Earn money from Facebook watch-

While using Facebook, you must have seen many features that you will also be using and there will be some features about which you will have a little idea about or which you may not know about.

Many of these features are such that can become your source of income and are becoming very popular too.

You must have seen a feature on your Facebook which is called Facebook Watch.

But there will be many of you who do not know about them, so in this article you are going to know everything about Facebook Watch.

Facebook Watch is a service that provides different types of video streaming service.

Although you will get this feature on other websites as well, but on Facebook also you can earn money by using this feature.

This service is specially made for video content creators in which videos can be uploaded.

Its popularity is very high because every video creator has started using it, due to which they also get their hard earned money.

Therefore, it is a very good tool for those who want to earn money from this feature.

Under this you will get many facilities.

Facebook Watch gives its users recommendations according to their choice, where you can easily contact and subscribe to people through the Show Link group.

Under this, you get the option to like and comment, even you can do real time chat with your friend or vivar.

Under this, no one will have to search for new videos because this video makes new videos available to you in the news feed itself.

This is a very good option for the creator publisher, from which they can earn money, but under this you will also get some conditions, which you can take advantage of only after you advance, which are as follows-

1. The biggest condition to join Facebook Watch is that you must have a Facebook page where there must be 10000 active audience.

2. Along with this, the creators will have to be active on Facebook for at least 90 days.

3. When you create a video, its length should be 3 minutes or more.

4. There is also a condition that at least ☐ 30000 should come on your videos within 2 months and at least 1 minute or more of that video should be seen.

You can earn money from Facebook Watch only after you are aware of these conditions.

Now this question must be coming in the mind of many people that what kind of videos are played in Facebook Watch, which get money?

So the way ads run on YouTube videos, in the same way ads run on Facebook Watch.

Millions of people are using Facebook and uploading their videos.

If you upload a video to Facebook Watch, it appears directly on the News Feed where the user does not have to search to see the video.

Under this there is a feedback option where people who watch and like your videos in Facebook Watch give you feedback from where you earn.

However, under this you can also earn money in other ways such as affiliate marketing and URL shortener etc.

Because Facebook is a very big company, it is imperative for millions of people to be active here every day and this gives a lot of benefit to the marketer.

There may be many people who can sponsor you to promote your product on your Facebook watch which you can show on Facebook watch by creating a creative ad and get commission.

Maybe in the coming times, Facebook Watch may become a feature that will become more popular than a channel like YouTube.

At present, Facebook does not have many features like channels like YouTube, but keeping in mind the growing technology, it can be said that Facebook will become even more popular in the coming times and where it supports only a few devices. Can support all devices.

That's why crores of people are using this feature imagining the future.

While using Facebook Watch, you have to take care of all the conditions mentioned by it and also keep in mind that you know everything about this feature very well.

The better you know about this feature, the easier it will be for you to use it.

Once you know about it and learn to use it properly, then you can earn a lot.

If you start working according to the interest of the people, then you will get more benefit.

23

5. Earn money by becoming an account manager on Facebook-

In Facebook, you must have seen many accounts in which there are millions of followers and the work of those people is also very big and spread and because of this they face problems in handling the account.

Therefore, those people who can not manage their account, they can manage their account for such people and for this they are also ready to pay money.

Millions of people are connected to each other in Facebook, so when they have a lot of followers in their account, then they also take out such a vacancy to manage Facebook account in which they need account manager or Facebook Ads manager. And you yourself can also contact such people because the number of such people on Facebook is very high.

To do this work, you should have all the information related to it well like you should know how to post and promote.

If you think that you have good knowledge of all these then you can easily earn money by doing this work.

Social media account manager gets a good salary, you just have to keep in mind that the work done by you should be liked by the owner of the account and your work should be unique.

Every work done by you should be beneficial for the company only then you can earn money by becoming a good Facebook account manager.

The most work that is done under this is to manage ads.

If you have good knowledge of ad management then it is even more beneficial for you.

Under Facebook, you will find an ad manager tool, under which you can manage ads.

You can set up, view and change the ad across all your Facebook campaigns and get its results as well.

Many companies resort to advertisements for the promotion of their products and brands, so if you start doing this work by joining those companies, then you can earn up to 50 thousand rupees a month.

Nowadays, many celebrities, political leaders and small and big companies are also looking for Facebook account manager to further their work on social media because they do not have enough time to do this work themselves.

Those people look for a client who is able to manage their account and can also face all kinds of problems, so people who have this skill can manage Facebook account in many ways and this work full time. And part time can be done both ways.

Most of the people need a manager who is very creative so if you are interested in ad designing then you can design and create ad in step by step process and use it.

Once you've created your ad, you post it on the company's page and you can set the location within it.

If you give the right information about the advertisement, then the company concerned will benefit more from it, so that you will be called a great account manager and you may also get more benefit from the company concerned.

The job of the account manager is to attract the audience to himself and at the same time you have to take care of the budget of the company.

In addition, you may also need to provide a report on the performance of your ad to the relevant company.

Keep an eye on the performance of your advertising and your schedule from time to time, so that you can do analysis and get a better result for the company.

It is the job of Facebook Ads Manager to get maximum profit for the company by running ads on Facebook, which is also very easy, just you should have knowledge of Facebook feature.

This is a very good option to make your career.

27

6. Earn money by freelancing in Facebook-

In today's era, everyone wants to earn money sitting at home because today technology has facilitated everyone that they can work online only by managing their time and more money than they cannot earn from traditional work through digital marketing. can earn.

That's why everyone wants that they should also have such a means that they can earn money sitting at home and they do not have to work under anyone, that is, they themselves are their own boss.

The method which gives you the opportunity to earn money sitting at home is freelancing and you must have heard about it as it has become a popular medium.

As you know that by freelancing you can earn money by managing your time sitting at home and nowadays its demand has also become very high, so if you want, you can do freelancing work using a famous platform like Facebook.

Facebook is a very big platform, so you will find crores of people here who pay for freelancing work because nowadays there is an era of website and internet, so there is a lot of demand for freelancing jobs like web developer, logo designing, graphic designing and content writing. But you will see.

Any client who is looking for a worker for freelancing work, either they go to the website of freelance work or else they mostly search on Facebook.

In such a situation, if you promote on Facebook by creating a solid profile, then you can get a good way of earning through Facebook.

Facebook is a trusted app that has made freelancing work very popular.

Freelancing work is the work in which a person works for himself instead of working under a company and is responsible for all kinds of things, he only associates with companies and projects given by them. Completes and receives payment.

The demand for freelancing is very high and this work is easily available on Facebook.

Inside it you will find many jobs in which you can work according to your interest.

It is very easy to do freelancing work in Facebook because for this you only need to know the things in which you want to work.

Under freelancing work, you can do many things such as – graphic design, copywriting, photography, editing, developing web designing, translator and many more options will be available to you.

First of all, to start freelancing work, you have to choose the best platform such as- Facebook.

Because here crores of people take out vacancies of this kind of work.

In Facebook, you have to make a good and strong profile of yourself so that people can be attracted towards you.

In your profile, you have to write every information related to your work, such as - what kind of work do you do? How much experience do you have with it? How much do you charge for it?

You will find many projects on Facebook and based on these projects you will work for which you will get money.

You can get paid for this work by the hour, day, week or month.

To do freelancing work, you will start with the right details as per your qualification.

After creating your profile, you have to join such group in Facebook which is related to your work.

For example, if you work as a translator, then you have to join the group associated with the translator.

Keep in mind that you join such a group in which more and more people are connected because by doing so the chances of fraud are very less.

Many times it may happen that clients give you a project after seeing your earlier work, so if you want to get big projects, then for that you have to keep in mind that your work is unique and away from all kinds of mistakes.

It can be difficult to find work in the beginning, it takes a long time to contact multiple companies, send them emails and wait for their reply.

Therefore, on Facebook, you can directly contact those people who get such work done and it does not take much time.

When you contact these people on Facebook, new projects will start coming to you.

Suppose if you do writing work then you can charge money according to the number of words.

If your clients like your work, you can increase your value over time.

If you are creative then freelancing work is very beneficial for you and on Facebook you will get all kinds of freelancing work groups available where you can work for many people simultaneously.

Once clients start coming to you and they like your work, then you can earn a lot of money by freelancing.

Keep posting posts related to your work on Facebook continuously so that your post reaches more and more people and they can know that you also do freelancing work.

If you want, you can post an article written by you on Facebook or a sample of any freelancing work done by you.

So that the client can read it and know how your work is.

This increases the chances of getting the project.

One advantage of freelancing is that there is no dearth of work because in this era of internet and technology, new options are being born, so the work of freelancing can reach even more heights in future. You will not lack any work under this, so freelancing is considered to be the best way to make a career.

7. Earn money by shortening the URL-

Do you want that you get a chance to earn more money in less effort but you are not able to find the right guide line for that?

So here you will come to know about such a way, using which you can earn a lot of money on Facebook, that too by doing very little hard work.

Have you seen any such link on the Internet which is very small in appearance but when you click on it, it becomes very big and whatever tax is present under it completely changes.

Do you know what it is and how it happens?

If not then let me tell you that it is called short URL which is used to shorten the website link.

This is a work by which you can earn money too.

By using this on your Facebook, you can earn a lot because there are many people on Facebook who pay to shorten the URL.

All you need to know is how to shorten URL and how to use it on Facebook.

This task is very easy, for this you just have to copy the link of a website, after copying which you will go to Google and go there and type the URL shortener.

You will see that many websites will be available in front of you and you can use any of these websites.

Now you go to any website, there you will see the option to paste the URL where you have to paste your link and click on the shortener.

After doing this, you will be given a short URL by that website which you will have to copy and keep.

You have to contact people on your Facebook account who pay for URL shortening.

If you are already doing website link sharing, then most of you have to shorten the URL, but very few people know that money can also be earned by using it.

There are many such groups on Facebook where you will find people who pay you for shortening the URL because today's world is the world of advertising.

Whenever you get a client, you just have to shorten the URL and copy and share it, as many people click on your short URL, they will see an ad from which you will get money.

Where the thing to keep in mind is that whenever someone clicks on your short URL, they will first see the advertisement, later the content or any information will be visible.

Apart from this, keep in mind that you cannot share the link of the paid URL shortener website on Facebook.

If questions are still arising in your mind, then we give you an example and explain how you can earn money by using it-

Suppose you share the link of a video with your friends, for which you have to copy and paste it and share it with your friends, but if you share this link by shortening the URL, then you get paid for it. Huh.

Similarly, on Facebook, you can share the links of many websites by shortening it, so that you will get money according to every single click on it.

The way to earn money by sharing short links on Facebook page is very easy and popular and for this you just have to create a Facebook page on Facebook and do a little work on that page to increase followers.

To earn more on Facebook, you share as many good content as possible to people, such as a big platform like YouTube, where millions of people are present and many good videos are available to you, you can make a good income by using it.

For example, you can shorten a video of YouTube and post it on the Facebook page.

Along with this, copy the link of that video by shortening it through a URL shortenn website.

When people start liking the short video of your Facebook page, then they will definitely demand full video from you and then you share the short link of that video on your page.

When people click on that link, an ad will come in front of them and only after watching that ad completely they will be able to watch the full video and you will get its money.

In this way you can earn money by using URL shortening, this method is also becoming popular nowadays because it takes less effort and many such websites are also available from which you can do URL shortening work for free.

8. Earn money by creating Facebook group and Facebook page-

Ways to earn money from Facebook also includes Facebook pages and Facebook groups.

For this you need an audience on your page.

If you have a large audience on your account, then you can easily earn money using Facebook pages and groups.

After gathering an audience on Facebook Pages and Facebook Groups, you will need to engage with some marketing sources such as affiliate marketing, promotion and advertising, product sales or audience networks

When you connect with these sources, you can earn a lot of money through them.

So let us tell you one by one how you can use your Facebook group and your Facebook page to earn money.

1. We have already told you about affiliate marketing, in which you have to share only its link on your page.

Example: You must have heard the name of Meesho app, it is an online store where you will get to see everything related to fashion.

If you join this company then you can promote their product on your Facebook page or Facebook group.

First of all you have to join this company and get an affiliate link from this company which you will link in your Facebook page or Facebook group and when any user in your page or your group will buy the product by clicking on it then you will get the price of that product. will get 10% of the

2. If you have such group or page on Facebook in which 10000 members are present, then you can earn money through direct sponsorship by sharing logo ad and video ad of any brand or website on the page.

If you have millions of likes on your page, then such people will contact you themselves who want to advertise their brand or product and if you do not have more likes or members on your page, then you yourself can contact those people by going to the online marketplace There are those who do the work of giving advertisements, in this way you can earn money by showing ads on your page.

Both the methods mentioned here are very popular, through which one can easily earn from 5 thousand to 10 thousand rupees every month.

9. Earn money by promoting YouTube channel on Facebook-

Both Facebook and YouTube are such big platforms that the communication level of both is huge.

Millions of people use both these platforms, so just imagine how much benefit you can get if these two platforms become one.

If you have a popular group on Facebook that has a lot of audience, then you can take good advantage of it, in which one advantage is that you can promote YouTube channel on it.

Under this, you can increase traffic to the blog or website by promoting your own channel and if you want to do this work for them by taking money from someone else, then it can become a very good way to make your career.

You must have seen in YouTube that crores of people post many videos every day, on which many people have millions of audiences on their channels and there are also many such channels which have very less audience.

To overcome this problem, you can promote your YouTube channel or someone else's YouTube channel on your Facebook page and earn money.

Here we are going to tell you how you can earn maximum by promoting YouTube channel on Facebook and bring audience to your YouTube channel.

Do you have a YouTube channel and you are worried about the audience not coming to your channel?

If yes, then you will get the solution of your problem in this article.

Here you can not only bring audience to your YouTube channel through Facebook but you can also earn money by promoting in Facebook.

Facebook is such a big platform that there are crores of users here, so promoting here can be a very good medium to bring audience to YouTube channel.

It is mostly seen that makers of videos in YouTube channel share the link of their videos on Facebook, but this does not benefit them much and also takes a lot of time.

But here you will find a way through which your YouTube video will be automatically uploaded on Facebook and in this way you will get audience on both the platforms and you will benefit.

So let's know how we can link our YouTube channel with Facebook-

First of all you have to use Chrome browser or any other browser and before using it, you should set your Facebook in classic mod.

Now you must be thinking that why can't we do this work through Facebook?

So let us tell you that if you use the Facebook app, then you will not get all the features using which you can link your YouTube to Facebook and your Facebook should be in classic mode for this to work.

So let's tell you step by step how to do YouTube calling on Facebook from which you can earn your money.

1. First of all you have to login to Facebook with your ID and go to your page.

2. Now type YouTube tab in your Facebook search box and search.

3. When you do this, you will see many YouTube channels in which you have to click on the top one.

4. Now you will see the option of Use App in an interface on which you have to click

5. After this you have to select your Facebook page and click on Add page.

6. After this an option of YouTube will be added to your Facebook page which you will see in its menu.

7. When you click on YouTube, you will get the option of Application Settings. By going to this setting, you have to enter your YouTube channel ID.

8. After this, you will have to login to the YouTube channel which you have linked to Facebook, by going here you will go to the settings of your channel and click on Advanced Settings.

9. Here you will see User ID and Channel ID.

You have to copy and paste the channel ID in the YouTube tab of the Facebook page and save it.

After doing this your channel and FB account will be connected and whenever you upload your video on YouTube channel it will be automatically posted on Facebook page but it will not be visible to you on Facebook app.

In this way, you can earn a lot of money by using both the websites together for your marketing.

This is needed because whenever someone creates his new YouTube channel and wants to start his business through it, initially very few viewers come to his channel.

In such a situation, if you have linked your YouTube channel on Facebook, then it can be very beneficial for you.

This work is not full of hard work, just once you have linked the Facebook page to the YouTube channel, then you can link a lot sitting at home and bring traffic to your channel.

It also helps in saving your time and traffic is also well received.

However, you also have to pay attention to increasing the followers on your Facebook, so this method is very good for the marketer, because they get the audience on both the famous platform to sell their product and also get a good earning. goes.

Whenever someone sees and likes your videos on Facebook, then they will definitely go to your YouTube channel too.

In this way, a lot of benefit can be taken by connecting YouTube and Facebook.

Even if you do not do any business and want to earn money only by uploading a video on YouTube and bringing good views, then this method is very good and even if you have started selling a product on YouTube channel then this method is beneficial.

10. Earn Money Using Facebook Marketplace-

You must have heard about Facebook Marketplace.

This can also become a good source of income and if you are starting a business in which you want to sell your product or someone else's product and want to increase their sales, then using Facebook Marketplace you can do this work easily.

Here only you have to list your product in Facebook Marketplace.

If you want, you can also apply for promotion by putting some cost there, so that your product will reach different places through ads.

This question must also be coming in the mind of many people that what is Facebook Marketplace after all?

So let us tell you what is this feature after all?

Facebook Marketplace is a world wide public network and is a huge platform of social network, which provides the facility to the users to increase the sales of their products by connecting with the people in their area.

This feature has been added to Facebook a short time ago as a means of entering Facebook's new service.

It is called a marketplace because it is exactly like a market because the product can be easily transacted here.

As you know that with the increasing technology today people have also got this facility that they can easily do all the work sitting at home.

Whether it is online shopping or money transactions, you can do all these tasks on your smartphone.

There are many such websites on social media that do online buying and selling and now Facebook has also developed within itself and added a new feature marketplace, in which you can easily sell your product by entering its details and earn your income. can increase.

Facebook Marketplace feature is a digital market place where users connect with people in their area to buy and sell products, etc., where they get all the services.

Although one thing is worth noting that all the work of the transaction is done outside i.e. there is no legal responsibility of Facebook, here you work at your own risk.

Now it comes to how to make money using Facebook Marketplace and what is the way to use it?

So first let's know how to use Facebook Marketplace?

1. First of all open Facebook application on your mobile or laptop.

2. After this you will see three dots in the right side where you have to click.

3. As soon as you click on the three dots, a menu option will appear in front of you which appears with the Marketplace icon, all you have to do is go to it.

4. Now you have entered Facebook's Marketplace where you will find many options to sell and buy your products.

Under this, you get the option to search about any product.

You can sell from any category or location and here you also get the option to list your product.

It also has a camera function inside it, using which you can take images of the product and share it.

Under this, you can also see the messages about your transactions and talk to your customers at any time.

So by using these options in this way, you can take advantage of the Marketplace. Once you note that Facebook Marketplace is available for Android and iPhone users in the age group of 18 years and above.

Now you must have come to know what are the tasks you can do under Facebook Marketplace.

So now all you have to do is go ahead with your task and try to do all the transactions that you want to do.

Is the question coming in your mind that what can you buy or sell under this?

So let us tell you that under this you can sell small to big things like clothes, real estate items, TV, car etc.

Apart from this, there are many options through which you can start your business.

Under this the method of buying and selling is simple and you can easily get in touch with the people.

Whenever you sell any of your products through the Marketplace, keep in mind that that product complies with all the policies of Facebook.

The step you can take to avoid most fraud cases is to deliver your product to the customers only after receiving the full payment.

Also, in your caption, definitely write all the necessary things related to the product and also tell about its delivery time and status.

Use an option that is secure to receive payment.

In this way, by taking care of all the things, you can increase the sales of your product by using the Marketplace and earn a lot of money.

This feature provides you all the kind of service that a business needs.

This is a great feature of contacting customers, under which you do not even need much knowledge.

All you have to do is take care of Facebook's policy and your safety.

Along with this, you also have to keep in mind that your products should be such that according to the need of the people.

Apart from this, fix the price of your product to a limit so that people are attracted to you more and more and when you feel that you have made good customers then you can increase the price of your product.

Under the Facebook Market feature, you can send both new and old products, so this is a great feature.

Epilogue

So here you saw how you can earn money sitting at home using Facebook.

Using Facebook is very easy and by using it, you can take your business to a new level if you want.

This is such a tool that we use every day but never pay attention to how we can use this platform for our benefit.

There are many people who spend all their time just watching useless videos and posting posts.

Therefore, it is important that you use these platforms properly by using your time properly.

You will find many such examples who have built their business using social media platforms like Facebook.

Under this, you can increase the sale of any type of product and earn money.

If you are creative then it can be more beneficial for you because people like things made with your own hands.

Facebook has given a new look to the world of business today.

Many people use Facebook to sell their daily product and they also get profit.

You only need hard work because without hard work you cannot do any work.

You should have patience in this work.

If you go on thinking that you will get success in one night, then you will not be successful in doing any work.

There are millions and millions of people connected to Facebook, but it also takes some time for your product to reach them, so you need to be active on Facebook continuously.

You should be able to use all the features of Facebook well so that you can take advantage of every single feature to grow your business.

For this you need a complete guide which you have got in this blog.

If you have read this post carefully, then today you came to know about 10 such methods, which you might have heard about but never thought of using it.

So if you want to grow your business, then definitely try using it because Facebook has taken the business of many people to the heights, then maybe the next person is you.

So work hard and don't waste your time on this platform.

Try to use it properly.

Hope you liked today's post "How to earn money from Facebook" and will inspire you to move forward and also you must have got the answers to all your questions.

These were the easiest ways that we have shared with you, using them you can grow in business.

Stay connected with us for more such new online business ideas.

9 789356 109827

Printed by Libri Plureos GmbH in Hamburg,
Germany